iPHONE 16

Rumors, Expectations, Insights, and the Ultimate Guide to Mac Speculations and Surprises

Dive Deep into the Uncharted Waters of Apple's Next Masterpiece — Anticipate, Analyze, Amaze!

Tech Talker

Disclaimer

The information presented in this book is based on rumors, speculations, and insider insights surrounding the upcoming iPhone 16, scheduled for release in the fall of 2024. As of the time of writing, Apple has not officially confirmed the details mentioned herein.

It is important to note that the content of this book is speculative and subject to change. The technology landscape is dynamic, and details about upcoming products are often closely guarded by manufacturers. Apple, in particular, is known for keeping product details confidential until the official launch.

Due to the speculative nature of the information provided, there is a possibility that the features, design, and specifications of the iPhone 16 may differ from what is outlined in this book. Apple has the discretion to alter product details, add or remove features, and make adjustments based on various factors, including technological advancements, market trends, and internal considerations.

Readers are advised to stay updated with official announcements from Apple for the most accurate and reliable information about the iPhone 16. While this book aims to provide insights and expectations, it should not be considered a definitive source for the final product details.

The technology industry is characterized by rapid advancements and changes. New information, developments, or official statements from Apple may emerge after the publication of this book, impacting the accuracy of the content.

This book is an independent work and is not endorsed, sponsored, or affiliated with Apple Inc. The content is based on publicly available information, industry analysis, and speculations from various sources.

Readers are encouraged to use the information presented in this book as a basis for informed speculation and discussion. When making decisions related to purchasing or anticipating future products, it is recommended to rely on official announcements and verified sources.

The author acknowledges the limitations of relying on rumors and speculations and recognizes that the final product may differ significantly from the details provided in this book.

By proceeding to read this book, you acknowledge the speculative nature of its content and understand the inherent uncertainties associated with predicting the features and specifications of unreleased products.

Table of contents

Introduction

In the ever-evolving landscape of technology, one company stands as the vanguard of innovation, teasing us with glimpses of the future. Apple, the maestro of groundbreaking devices, is ready to unveil its next masterpiece — the iPhone 16. As we stand on the precipice of anticipation, this book invites you to join a journey into the realms of speculation, whispers, and the untold tales surrounding the much-anticipated iPhone 16.

Picture this: a world where every tap, swipe, and interaction with your device is not just a task but a symphony of seamless brilliance. The iPhone 16, a creation shrouded in mystery, whispers promises of an unparalleled user experience and technological marvels yet unseen.

This isn't just a book; it's a portal into the heart of Apple's innovation, a voyage into the uncharted waters of what might be. As you turn these pages, let the thrill of anticipation ignite your curiosity and fan the flames of wonder. We are not merely observers; we are explorers, navigating the labyrinth of rumors, expectations, and insights that pave the way to Apple's next revelation.

In this narrative, we embark on a quest to decipher the secrets hidden within the whispers of insiders, the leaks from Apple's innovation lab, and the speculative musings of tech enthusiasts worldwide. Brace yourself for a rollercoaster of excitement, as we delve into the potential features, design innovations, and technological leaps that the iPhone 16 might bring.

So, dear reader, fasten your seatbelt and prepare to be mesmerized. The journey into the heart of iPhone 16 begins here, where anticipation meets revelation, and the future is but a turn of the page away. Welcome to the captivating saga of the iPhone 16 — a journey that transcends the ordinary and invites you to witness the extraordinary.

As we unravel the mysteries within, remember, it's not just about the device; it's about the stories it holds, the possibilities it unlocks, and the anticipation it ignites. Let the adventure commence.

Chapter 1:

The iPhone 16 Lineup

In the ever-expanding realm of technological marvels, the iPhone 16 is poised to redefine our expectations, not just in features but also in size. Apple, known for pushing the boundaries of innovation, is gearing up to introduce larger dimensions to its iconic iPhone lineup.

The iPhone 16 Pro is set to undergo a transformation, growing in stature to a remarkable 6.3 inches. This marks a significant departure from the familiar, heralding the dawn of a new era for Pro enthusiasts. Picture a display that immerses you in a world of vibrant colors, intricate details, and seamless interactions, all encapsulated within the palm of your hand.

Taking the crown of grandeur, the iPhone 16 Pro Max outshines its predecessors with a colossal 6.9-inch display. Apple's commitment to delivering an expansive and immersive user experience is epitomized in the Max model. Bigger, bolder, and undeniably beautiful, the Pro Max promises a visual feast that transcends the boundaries of ordinary smartphone dimensions.

In a strategic move, Apple has chosen to maintain the size integrity of the standard iPhone 16 and iPhone 16 Plus, aligning them with the dimensions of their iPhone 15 counterparts. This decision ensures that users who prefer the familiar feel of their current devices can seamlessly transition to the latest models without compromising on size.

Let's delve into the specifics:

iPhone 16 Pro:
- Thickness: 8.25 mm
- Height: 149.6 mm
- Width: 71.45 mm
- Display: 6.3 inches (159.31 mm)
- Weight: 194 grams

iPhone 16 Pro Max:
- Thickness: 8.25 mm
- Height: 163.0 mm
- Width: 77.58 mm

- Display: 6.9 inches (174.06 mm)
- Weight: 225 grams

These dimensions are not just numbers; they are a gateway to an unparalleled visual experience. The larger sizes of the iPhone 16 Pro and Pro Max models are not merely about grandeur; they are about immersing yourself in a canvas of innovation, where every pixel tells a story, and every interaction is a masterpiece.

New design prototypes and their potential impact

In the secretive corridors of Apple's design labs, where innovation meets imagination, the iPhone 16 is taking shape in multiple prototypes, each a testament to the pursuit of perfection. These prototypes offer a glimpse into the future, showcasing potential design revolutions that could redefine our relationship with technology.

One of the prototypes adopts a pill-shaped iPhone X-style camera design. Picture a sleek, elongated module housing cutting-edge optics. This design not only adds a touch of sophistication but also hints at advancements in camera capabilities. Aesthetic meets functionality in a harmonious dance, setting the stage for a visual renaissance.

Two other prototypes take a different route, featuring distinctive dual-lens designs. One integrates haptic buttons with a unified volume button, offering a seamless tactile experience.

The other prototype embraces the traditional mechanical volume buttons, introducing an "Action Button" and a novel "Capture Button." This variation promises versatility, catering to both classic preferences and a thirst for innovation.

Within these prototypes lies a feature that transcends the ordinary – a periscope zoom lens. Imagine unlocking a world of optical wonders, bringing distant details closer with precision and clarity. This addition not only elevates the photographic prowess of the iPhone 16 but also positions it as a pioneer in mobile photography innovation.

The design explorations extend beyond functionality to aesthetics. The renders showcase colors that Apple has tested, teasing the possibility of a palette that includes pink, yellow, and black for the standard iPhone 16 models. This isn't just a phone; it's a canvas waiting to be personalized, reflecting your style and personality.

As we navigate the landscape of prototypes, one design emerges as the likely choice. Featuring a vertically aligned rear camera, it introduces a second "Capture" button on the right side for video recording, coupled with a left-side mmWave antenna in the United States, strategically positioned below the Action Button.

These design prototypes aren't merely cosmetic variations; they are blueprints for a revolution. The chosen design promises a harmonious marriage of form and function, where aesthetics seamlessly integrate with technological prowess. The periscope zoom lens hints at a leap in photography capabilities, while the color options open the door to personal expression.

In-depth analysis of the vertically aligned camera layout

In the intricate dance of technology and design, the iPhone 16 introduces a pivotal shift – a vertically aligned camera layout. This deliberate choice by Apple is not merely aesthetic; it's a strategic fusion of form and function, a canvas where innovation meets intentionality.

The Visual Symphony

1. Spatial Mastery with Vertical Alignment

The vertically aligned camera layout isn't just a visual spectacle; it's a key to unlocking spatial mastery. Positioned vertically, the camera lenses offer a unique perspective, paving the way for spatial video recording capabilities. Imagine capturing moments in three-dimensional richness, a feature set to elevate your content creation experience to unprecedented heights.

2. Aesthetic Harmony with Symmetry

Beyond functionality, the vertical alignment introduces a sense of symmetry and balance to the iPhone 16's design. Each lens, each element contributes to a visual harmony that transcends the utilitarian aspects of a smartphone. It's not just about capturing images; it's about creating visual poetry.

The Technical Symphony

1. Enhanced Stability in Capture

The vertical alignment inherently enhances the stability of the camera system, especially during handheld captures. This design choice minimizes the chances of unintentional tilting or misalignment, ensuring that every shot is a masterpiece of stability and clarity.

2. Spatial Video: A Glimpse into the Future

With the vertically aligned lenses, the iPhone 16 is poised to pioneer spatial video recording. This technology captures depth and dimension, adding a layer of realism to your videos. It's not just recording; it's capturing moments in a way that makes you feel present, as if you can step into the memories you create.

The Human Symphony

1. Intuitive Interaction: Capture Button Placement

The chosen vertical alignment sets the stage for an intuitive interaction experience. Placing the new "Capture Button" on the right side aligns with the natural grip of the hand, ensuring that capturing photos and videos becomes a seamless extension of your creative impulses.

2. Merging Functionality: mmWave Antenna Integration

The spatial design isn't limited to the camera alone. The vertically aligned rear camera is complemented by a left-side mmWave antenna in the United States, strategically positioned below the Action Button. This integration not only enhances connectivity but also showcases Apple's commitment to a holistic and cohesive design.

As we dissect the intricacies of the iPhone 16's vertically aligned camera layout, it becomes clear that this is more than a visual choice – it's a symphony. It's the harmony of aesthetics, functionality, and human interaction, all orchestrated to redefine how we perceive and interact with the world through our smartphones.

Chapter 2:

A-series Chips and Performance

In the heart of Apple's relentless pursuit of technological excellence lies the beating heart of the iPhone 16 – the A-series chips. These chips, built on the cutting-edge N3E 3-nanometer node, are poised to redefine the boundaries of performance, efficiency, and innovation.

The N3E Revolution

1. N3E 3-nanometer Node

The iPhone 16's A-series chips represent a leap into the future with the adoption of the N3E 3-nanometer node. This technological marvel is not just a reduction in size; it's a paradigm shift. The N3E node brings unprecedented levels of efficiency, allowing for more transistors to be packed into a smaller space, resulting in enhanced performance without compromising on power consumption.

2. Efficiency Redefined

At the core of the N3E node's impact is a redefinition of efficiency. The A-series chips on the N3E node promise to deliver more computational power per watt, ensuring that every task, from the mundane to the demanding, is executed with finesse. It's not just about raw power; it's about optimizing every ounce of energy for a seamless user experience.

The A-series Symphony

1. The A17 Chip

The iPhone 16 and iPhone 16 Plus are set to be powered by the formidable A17 chip. This powerhouse is not a mere iteration but a revelation, representing the pinnacle of Apple's chip design prowess. The A17 chip, with its roots in the N3E 3-nanometer node, is geared to elevate speed, responsiveness, and overall performance to new heights.

2. A18 Series for the Pro Models

While the standard iPhone 16 models boast the A17 chip, the Pro models are rumored to house the A18 and A18 Pro chips. This nuance in nomenclature signifies that Apple is not merely following a linear progression but introducing distinct variations tailored for the Pro models. The Pro chips could potentially feature an extra GPU core, adding an extra layer of prowess for demanding tasks.

The Fusion of Art and Engineering

1. Thermal Alchemy: Graphene Thermal System

The iPhone 16 isn't just about raw power; it's about sustainability. To combat overheating concerns, Apple is venturing into uncharted territory with a graphene thermal system. Graphene, with its exceptional thermal conductivity, promises to dissipate heat effectively, ensuring that the iPhone 16 remains cool even under the most demanding tasks.

2. RAM Upgrade:

Equipped with 8GB of RAM, the standard iPhone 16 models are geared to handle multitasking with ease. This upgrade from the iPhone 15 models ensures that the iPhone 16 doesn't just meet expectations; it surpasses them, providing a seamless and responsive user experience.

As we unravel the insights into the latest A-series chips on the N3E 3-nanometer node, it becomes evident that the iPhone 16 is not just a smartphone; it's a symphony of technology and artistry. The N3E revolutionizes efficiency, the A-series chips redefine performance, and the additional features like the graphene thermal system and increased RAM elevate the iPhone 16 to a new echelon of excellence.

Expectations for improved efficiency and performance

In the ever-evolving landscape of smartphone technology, Apple's commitment to pushing the boundaries is exemplified in the iPhone 16. As we anticipate the upcoming release, expectations soar high, especially in the realms of efficiency and performance. Let's unravel the intricacies that promise to make the iPhone 16 a beacon of technological excellence.

1. N3E 3-nanometer Node:

At the core of the iPhone 16's promise is the adoption of the N3E 3-nanometer node. This technological marvel isn't just a leap; it's a quantum leap. The reduction in size not only contributes to a more compact and sleek design but, more importantly, it signifies a surge in efficiency. More transistors in a smaller space mean enhanced computational power with minimized energy consumption, setting the stage for a device that effortlessly balances performance and longevity.

2. A17 Chip:

The beating heart of the iPhone 16, the A17 chip, emerges as a symbol of Apple's dedication to performance. Beyond raw power, the A17 chip is engineered for efficiency. It's not just about handling demanding tasks with speed; it's about doing so with finesse, ensuring that every operation, from the mundane to the resource-intensive, is executed seamlessly. The fusion of the N3E node and the A17 chip is a testament to Apple's pursuit of the perfect balance between power and efficiency.

3. Graphene Thermal System:

Efficiency extends beyond computational power; it's about sustainability in every aspect. The introduction of the graphene thermal system in the iPhone 16 is a stride toward maintaining optimal operating temperatures. Graphene's exceptional thermal conductivity promises effective heat dissipation, ensuring that the iPhone 16 remains cool even during prolonged and resource-intensive usage. It's not just about peak performance; it's about consistent and reliable efficiency.

4. RAM Upgrade:

In the realm of multitasking, the iPhone 16 stands poised to redefine user expectations. With a substantial upgrade to 8GB of RAM, the standard models of the iPhone 16 are geared to handle multiple applications simultaneously. This isn't just a numerical increment; it's a strategic enhancement that guarantees a seamless and responsive user experience. The efficiency of RAM management ensures that the iPhone 16 doesn't just meet but surpasses the demands of modern, dynamic usage patterns.

5. Symphony of Components:

The beauty of efficiency in the iPhone 16 lies not in isolated elements but in the orchestrated symphony of components. The N3E node, A17 chip, graphene thermal system, and upgraded RAM aren't disparate features; they're integral notes in a harmonious composition. Each element plays a crucial role in crafting a device that is not only powerful but consistently efficient, adapting to the diverse needs of its users.

6. User-Centric Innovation:

Ultimately, the expectations for improved efficiency and performance in the iPhone 16 are rooted in the desire for a seamless user experience. It's about a device that doesn't just keep up with the demands of modern life but anticipates and exceeds them. As we await the unveiling of the iPhone 16, the anticipation isn't just for a smartphone; it's for a technological marvel that seamlessly integrates into our lives, enhancing efficiency and performance in ways that redefine our digital experiences.

The Mysterious Extra Button and its Speculated Functionalities

In the realm of smartphone innovation, every button, and every feature is meticulously designed to enhance user experience. However, in the upcoming iPhone 16, a new addition to the physical interface has sparked curiosity and speculation—the mysterious extra button.

As we embark on the journey to unravel its secrets, we delve into the speculated functionalities that this enigmatic button might bring to the table.

1. The Capture Button:

Positioned strategically on the same side as the power button, the extra button, internally referred to as the "Capture Button," introduces a realm of creative possibilities. This capacitive button isn't just an accessory; it's a portal for users to capture moments in a way that transcends the conventional. By detecting both pressure and touch, the Capture Button is poised to redefine the photography and videography experience on the iPhone 16.

2. Pressure-Sensitive Photography:

The integration of pressure sensitivity in the Capture Button opens doors to a new dimension of photography. Imagine adjusting the focus or zoom of your camera not just through taps and swipes but by subtly varying the pressure applied to the Capture Button. It's a tactile and intuitive approach to photography that promises a more hands-on and immersive experience, allowing users to unleash their creativity with a simple touch.

3. Zooming with Precision:

Zooming in on details becomes an art form with the speculated haptic feedback feature of the Capture Button. As users press and adjust the pressure on the button, the haptic feedback provides a nuanced response, allowing for precise control over zoom levels. It's not just about capturing an image; it's about crafting it with precision, ensuring that every shot is a masterpiece shaped by the user's artistic intent.

4. Seamless Video Capture:

Video enthusiasts are in for a treat with the Capture Button's rumored functionalities. By combining touch sensitivity with pressure detection, users can seamlessly transition between capturing photos and recording videos. The tactile nature of the button adds a layer of control to video recording, empowering users to compose and capture cinematic moments with a level of finesse previously unmatched in smartphone videography.

5. Integration with AI:

Beyond the physical mechanics, the Capture Button is speculated to integrate with the iPhone 16's AI capabilities. This synergy opens avenues for smart capture functionalities, where the device intelligently analyzes scenes and adjusts settings based on user preferences. The Capture Button becomes more than a physical interface; it becomes a conduit for users to communicate their creative vision to the device, with AI serving as a collaborative partner in the photographic process.

6. Awaiting Discovery

As we navigate the realm of rumors and speculations, the true potential of the mysterious extra button in the iPhone 16 remains unseen. It's a canvas of possibilities, waiting for users to uncover and redefine how they interact with their devices. The Capture Button isn't just a button; it's a tactile adventure, an exploration of innovative possibilities that promises to reshape the way we engage with the art of capturing moments on our smartphones.

Chapter 3:

Design Innovations

In the ever-evolving landscape of smartphone design, the iPhone 16 is poised to introduce a groundbreaking feature that goes beyond the surface – the integration of solid-state volume buttons.

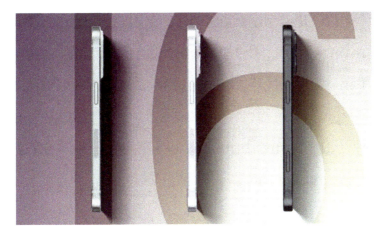

This departure from conventional physical buttons signifies not just a shift in aesthetics but a leap forward in user experience. Let's embark on a journey to unravel the nuances and advantages that solid-state volume buttons bring to the iPhone 16.

As we bid farewell to the familiar clicks associated with traditional buttons, the iPhone 16's solid-state volume buttons promise a tactile experience redefined. The transition to haptic feedback introduces a touch of sophistication, creating a seamless interaction that extends beyond mere functionality. The elegance of the haptic response is not only pleasing to the senses but also contributes to a refined and modern user experience.

One of the standout advantages of solid-state volume buttons lies in their resilience against environmental elements. Unlike their mechanical counterparts, which are susceptible to water and dust damage, solid-state buttons operate through touch and pressure sensitivity. This design choice enhances the iPhone 16's durability, making it more adaptable to various conditions. Users can confidently navigate their device without the concern of potential damage to the volume controls.

The space-efficient design of solid-state buttons contributes to a sleek and modern aesthetic for the iPhone 16. With no need for physical depressions or dedicated spaces for button movements, Apple gains flexibility in crafting a device that is not just technologically advanced but also visually appealing. The result is a smartphone that embodies a contemporary design philosophy, setting it apart in a world of evolving expectations.

The capacitive nature of solid-state volume buttons brings forth a new level of tactile precision. Users can expect a nuanced control over volume levels, adjusting with a finesse that surpasses the binary nature of traditional buttons. Each touch is registered with accuracy, providing a responsive and satisfying interaction. This enhanced tactile experience contributes to the overall pleasure of using the iPhone 16, elevating the user interface to new heights.

Beyond the immediate advantages, the introduction of solid-state volume buttons aligns with Apple's commitment to a unified user experience across devices. As this technology becomes a standard feature in Apple's ecosystem, users can seamlessly transition between adjusting volumes on their iPhone, iPad, or other compatible devices. This harmonization reinforces Apple's dedication to user-centric design, ensuring consistency and familiarity across the ecosystem.

Looking ahead, the adoption of solid-state volume buttons in the iPhone 16 is not merely a feature; it's a statement of adaptability and innovation. Apple sets a standard for future devices, anticipating the evolving landscape of user interaction. The solid-state revolution in volume control isn't just a technological upgrade; it's a testament to Apple's continuous quest to redefine the way users engage with their devices.

As we anticipate the unveiling of the iPhone 16, the incorporation of solid-state volume buttons emerges as a pivotal moment – a testament to Apple's unwavering commitment to pushing the boundaries of design and functionality. The tactile elegance, durability, and precision offered by these buttons herald a new era in smartphone interaction, inviting users to experience the future of technology in their hands.

The "Capture" button for enhanced photo and video capabilities

In the dynamic realm of smartphone innovation, the iPhone 16 is poised to redefine the way we capture and immortalize moments with the introduction of the revolutionary "Capture" button. This game-changing feature transcends the traditional boundaries of photography and videography, promising users an unprecedented level of control and creativity. Let's delve into the intricacies of this innovative addition, exploring how the "Capture" button is set to elevate the iPhone 16's photo and video capabilities to new heights.

Imagine a button dedicated solely to capturing the essence of a moment, a button strategically placed to enhance your photographic and videographic endeavors. The "Capture" button on the iPhone 16 is not just a physical element; it's a gateway to unlocking a world of possibilities. Nestled conveniently within reach, this button transforms the act of capturing memories into a seamless and intuitive experience.

The primary function of the "Capture" button is to provide users with a dedicated shortcut for snapping photos and recording videos. No longer confined to tapping the screen or fumbling for on-screen controls, users can now access the "Capture" button with a single, instinctive press. This seemingly small adjustment holds the potential to revolutionize the spontaneity and immediacy of capturing life's fleeting moments.

Beyond its fundamental function, the "Capture" button on the iPhone 16 is designed for versatility. Users can expect an array of functionalities tied to this button, ranging from quick photo captures to instant video recording. Imagine effortlessly switching between capturing a breathtaking landscape in a still photo to seamlessly transitioning into recording a vibrant, action-packed moment—all at the touch of a button.

The tactile feedback of the "Capture" button adds an extra layer of engagement to the photography and videography experience. With a satisfying click, users receive immediate confirmation of their action, enhancing the overall sense of control and connection with their device. This tactile response is more than just a sensory delight; it's a deliberate design choice aimed at making the act of capturing content a more immersive and enjoyable process.

As we anticipate the arrival of the iPhone 16, the "Capture" button emerges as a catalyst for unleashing creativity. It empowers users to be in the moment, ready to capture life's unfolding stories with unprecedented ease. The strategic placement of the button and its seamless integration into the iPhone's design underscore Apple's commitment to user-centric innovation.

In the rapidly evolving landscape of smartphone technology, the "Capture" button is more than a feature; it's a testament to Apple's dedication to redefining the way we interact with our devices. It's an ode to the art of storytelling through visuals, an acknowledgment that every moment is worth capturing with precision and grace. The iPhone 16, with its innovative "Capture" button, invites users to be the authors of their visual narratives, ushering in a new era of creativity in mobile photography and videography.

Color options for the standard iPhone 16 models

As we journey into the enchanting realm of the upcoming iPhone 16, insider information offers us a sneak peek into the color palette that might grace the standard models. The anticipation is heightened with a glimpse into the renders created based on insider insights, adding an extra layer of credibility to the rumored hues.

According to the details sourced from an internal Apple informant who shared insights with MacRumors, the renders vividly depict the potential color options for the standard iPhone 16 models. Among the hues that Apple has purportedly tested, we could see a striking trio of colors: Pink, Yellow, and Black.

Imagine a sleek iPhone 16 in a sophisticated Midnight Black, radiating elegance and timeless appeal. Alternatively, visualize the playful vibrancy of a Coral or Electric Blue variant, adding a pop of personality to your device.

The renders not only provide a tantalizing glimpse into the potential color choices but also hint at the overall design aesthetics of the standard iPhone 16 models. As we eagerly await the official unveiling, let these leaked insights stoke the fires of anticipation for what promises to be a visually stunning addition to the iPhone lineup.

Chapter 4:

Display Technology

In the ever-evolving landscape of smartphone technology, the iPhone 16 is set to introduce a groundbreaking feature – micro-lens technology. This innovative addition to the OLED panels holds the promise of not only enhancing brightness but also revolutionizing power consumption.

The micro-lens technology is poised to create a significant impact on the display's brightness. By incorporating a uniform pattern of billions of lenses within the OLED panel, a phenomenon known as micro-lens arrays (MLA), Apple aims to reduce internal reflection. This reduction in reflection not only boosts perceived brightness but does so without a parallel increase in power consumption.

What sets micro-lens technology apart is its ability to offer improved brightness while simultaneously addressing power efficiency. The OLED displays featured in the iPhone 16 lineup are expected to benefit from this cutting-edge technology, ensuring that users experience a visually stunning display without compromising on battery life.

The iPhone 16's OLED panels, equipped with micro-lens arrays, represent a leap forward in display technology. These arrays contribute to the efficient use of light, allowing for a more vivid and power-efficient visual experience.

As we anticipate the official unveiling of the iPhone 16, the integration of micro-lens technology stands out as a testament to Apple's commitment to pushing the boundaries of what's possible. Join us on this exploration of the iPhone 16's features, where each innovation unfolds like a captivating chapter in the evolution of smartphones.

Power-efficient OLED displays for enhanced visual experience

In the realm of smartphone displays, the iPhone 16 is set to redefine the visual experience with its power-efficient OLED panels. These displays, meticulously designed and optimized, promise a visual symphony that balances stunning visuals with energy efficiency.

The OLED displays featured in the iPhone 16 are not just about vibrant colors and sharp contrasts; they are a testament to Apple's commitment to an enhanced visual experience without compromising on power efficiency. The technology behind these displays ensures a harmonious balance between captivating visuals and optimal energy consumption.

The power-efficient OLED panels go beyond conventional display technologies, offering users a display that is not only visually striking but also considerate of battery life. The optimization of power consumption contributes to a longer-lasting and sustainable usage experience.

Crafting power-efficient OLED displays involves a fusion of cutting-edge technology and meticulous engineering. Apple's dedication to pushing the boundaries of what's possible in display technology is evident in the iPhone 16, where every pixel comes alive with brilliance, and every interaction is a testament to efficiency.

Potential introduction of the iPhone 16 "Ultra" and its features

In the ever-evolving landscape of technological marvels, Apple is poised to introduce the iPhone 16 "Ultra," a device that transcends expectations and sets new standards for innovation. Let's embark on a journey to uncover the potential features that make the iPhone 16 "Ultra" a true beacon of cutting-edge technology.

The iPhone 16 "Ultra" is positioned as the apex of the iPhone lineup, boasting features that elevate performance to unprecedented heights. From advanced camera capabilities to a larger display, this device is designed for those who demand the absolute best in technology.

At the heart of the iPhone 16 "Ultra" experience lies a camera system that redefines smartphone photography. With additional camera improvements, enhanced low-light performance, and possibly a periscope zoom lens, users can expect a photography and videography powerhouse in the palm of their hands.

Featuring a larger display than its counterparts, the iPhone 16 "Ultra" promises an immersive visual experience. Whether it's streaming content, gaming, or productivity, the expansive screen real estate opens new possibilities, making every interaction a delight.

Rumors suggest that the iPhone 16 "Ultra" might embrace a portless design, eliminating traditional charging ports. This potential shift indicates Apple's commitment to a wireless future, offering users a seamless and streamlined experience.

Equipped with the latest connectivity features, the iPhone 16 "Ultra" could support Wi-Fi 7 technology, providing lightning-fast speeds and improved reliability. This ensures that users stay at the forefront of connectivity standards.

As we await the official unveiling, the iPhone 16 "Ultra" stands as a testament to Apple's relentless pursuit of excellence.

Chapter 5:

Connectivity

Adoption of Wi-Fi 7 for faster speeds and improved reliability

In a world where connectivity is king, Apple's iPhone 16 is poised to set a new standard with the adoption of Wi-Fi 7 technology. As we explore this groundbreaking feature, anticipate a leap forward in speeds, reliability, and the overall wireless experience.

Wi-Fi 7 is not just an incremental improvement; it's a giant leap in wireless technology. With speeds expected to reach "at least 30" gigabits per second, the iPhone 16 promises an unparalleled browsing, streaming, and downloading experience. Get ready to embrace a faster digital lifestyle.

Wi-Fi 7 introduces several technological advancements, including the ability to use 320MHz channels and support for 4K quadrature amplitude modulation (QAM) technology. These innovations translate to up to 2.4 times faster speeds compared to Wi-Fi 6, ensuring a seamless and responsive online experience.

The improved latency of Wi-Fi 7 means quicker response times for online activities. Whether you're gaming, video conferencing, or accessing cloud services, the iPhone 16 ensures minimal delays, providing a more immersive and real-time connection.

Wi-Fi 7 isn't just about speed; it's about creating a more reliable and stable connection. The technology is designed to handle crowded networks more efficiently, making it ideal for environments with multiple connected devices. Say goodbye to dropped connections and hello to a consistently robust signal.

While Wi-Fi 7 could potentially be a feature exclusive to the iPhone 16 Pro models, its introduction signifies Apple's commitment to keeping its devices at the forefront of connectivity standards. Stay ahead of the curve with a device that's not just current but future-ready.

As we eagerly await the official launch of the iPhone 16, the inclusion of Wi-Fi 7 is a testament to Apple's dedication to providing users with the best and most advanced technologies. Brace yourself for a wireless experience that redefines what's possible in the world of smartphones.

USB-C technology for enhanced connectivity

In a bold move towards universal compatibility, Apple is set to revolutionize the iPhone 16 with the adoption of USB-C technology.

This shift not only promises enhanced connectivity but also signifies a step towards a more standardized and versatile user experience.

Bid farewell to proprietary cables and adapters. The inclusion of USB-C in the iPhone 16 ensures compatibility with a wide range of devices and accessories. Whether you're connecting to your laptop, charging your phone, or transferring data, USB-C offers a one-size-fits-all solution.

USB-C is synonymous with faster charging speeds. With the iPhone 16, expect a significant boost in charging efficiency. Say goodbye to long waiting times for your device to power up, and embrace a charging experience that keeps up with your fast-paced lifestyle.

Transferring files between devices has never been faster. USB-C supports gigabit-speed data transfer, enabling quick and efficient sharing of large files, high-resolution videos, and more. Experience seamless data synchronization without the lag.

No more flipping the cable to find the right orientation – USB-C's reversible design makes it incredibly user-friendly. Plug in your cable effortlessly, whether in the dark or on the go, and enjoy a hassle-free connection experience.

USB-C is not just a charging port; it's a versatile interface that can support various functions. From connecting external displays to using peripherals like external storage devices, the iPhone 16's USB-C port opens up a world of possibilities.

As the iPhone 16 embraces USB-C, Apple reaffirms its commitment to delivering a user-friendly and forward-thinking smartphone experience. Get ready to embrace the future of connectivity with a device that not only keeps up with the times but sets the standard for what's to come.

Expected 5G modem chips for efficient and high-speed connectivity

Step into a new realm of connectivity with the iPhone 16, poised to redefine your smartphone experience through advanced 5G modem chips. Apple, at the forefront of technological innovation, ensures that the iPhone 16 is not just a device but a gateway to seamless, high-speed connectivity.

Anticipate a revolutionary shift in connectivity with the adoption of Qualcomm's Snapdragon X-series 5G modem chips in the iPhone 16. Known for their cutting-edge technology, these chips promise to deliver efficient and high-speed connectivity, ensuring that your iPhone 16 stays ahead in the fast-paced digital landscape.

The Snapdragon X-series brings a perfect blend of efficiency and speed to the iPhone 16. These modem chips are designed to optimize network performance, providing users with lightning-fast data speeds and a reliable connection. Whether you're streaming content, downloading files, or engaging in video calls, the Snapdragon X-series ensures a smooth and responsive experience.

Experience the power of advanced carrier aggregation, a key feature of Qualcomm's 5G modem technology. This innovative approach combines multiple carriers to boost data rates and enhance network capacity. The result? A faster and more reliable 5G connection that empowers your iPhone 16 to handle data-intensive tasks with ease.

The iPhone 16's adoption of Qualcomm's 5G modem chips ensures that you're future-proofed in the realm of connectivity. As networks evolve and 5G technology advances, your iPhone 16 will continue to deliver top-tier performance, keeping you connected to the latest and fastest networks available.

Prepare to witness the transformation of your digital experience as the iPhone 16 leverages the prowess of Qualcomm's Snapdragon X-series 5G modem chips. Connectivity will never be the same again—get ready to explore the endless possibilities that 5G brings to the palm of your hand.

Chapter 6:

User Interface Innovations

Embark on a tactile journey like never before with the introduction of solid-state technology for haptic buttons in the iPhone 16. Apple, synonymous with innovation, takes user interaction to new heights by incorporating cutting-edge solid-state haptic buttons, promising a seamless and responsive experience.

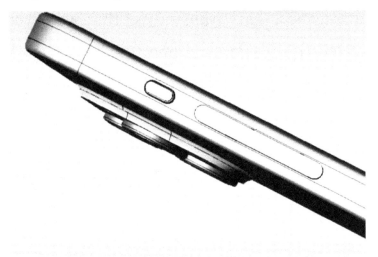

The iPhone 16 pioneers the use of solid-state technology for haptic buttons, breaking away from traditional mechanical buttons. This groundbreaking approach eliminates the physical movement of buttons, replacing it with a sophisticated haptic feedback system. Prepare to feel the future at your fingertips.

Solid-state haptic buttons bring a level of precision that transforms the way you interact with your iPhone 16. Each touch is met with a nuanced haptic vibration, mimicking the sensation of a physical button press. The result is a tactile experience that is not only accurate but also incredibly immersive.

Bid farewell to the wear and tear associated with traditional buttons. Solid-state technology enhances the durability and reliability of haptic buttons in the iPhone 16. The absence of moving parts means fewer points of failure, ensuring a prolonged lifespan for your device's interactive components.

Whether you're adjusting volume, powering off your device, or engaging with various functions, the solid-state haptic buttons in the iPhone 16 provide an immersive user experience. Feel the subtle feedback as you navigate through your device, creating a connection between you and your iPhone like never before.

Apple's integration of solid-state haptic buttons reaffirms its commitment to pushing the boundaries of innovation. The iPhone 16 not only embraces the future of interaction but also sets a new standard for user-centric design. Prepare to be captivated by the seamless, responsive, and futuristic feel of solid-state haptic buttons in the iPhone 16.

The expansion of the Action Button across the entire iPhone 16 lineup

In a bold move towards unified functionality, Apple takes a giant leap with the expansion of the Action Button across the entire iPhone 16 lineup. The Action Button, once exclusive to the Pro models, now becomes an integral part of every iPhone 16, promising a consistent and versatile user experience.

No longer confined to select models, the Action Button's expansion marks a departure from the norm, breaking down boundaries and ensuring that every iPhone 16 user can enjoy its multifaceted capabilities. Apple's commitment to inclusivity shines through as this powerful feature becomes a staple across the entire lineup.

The expanded Action Button seamlessly integrates into the design of each iPhone 16 variant, offering users a familiar and intuitive experience, irrespective of the model they choose. This move streamlines interactions and fosters a sense of continuity, ensuring that users can effortlessly harness the power of the Action Button across various tasks.

Originally introduced as a replacement for the traditional mute switch, the Action Button's expanded role extends beyond mere silencing functions. Across the iPhone 16 lineup, it serves as a dynamic tool for activating the flashlight, launching the camera, enabling or disabling Focus mode, triggering shortcuts, and much more. Versatility takes center stage as the Action Button becomes a catalyst for a myriad of actions.

Whether you opt for the standard iPhone 16 or the Pro models, the expanded Action Button guarantees a consistent user experience. Apple's dedication to user-centric design ensures that regardless of the device's specifications, the Action

Button becomes a reliable companion for various tasks, offering a sense of familiarity and ease of use.

As the Action Button becomes a standard feature, Apple positions the iPhone 16 lineup as not just a collection of devices but as a cohesive ecosystem of interconnected possibilities. This expansion is not merely about buttons; it's a testament to Apple's vision of the future, where user interaction is seamless, versatile, and, most importantly, consistently empowering.

Prepare to embark on a journey where every touch is an invitation to explore the expansive capabilities of the iPhone 16's Action Button. Apple's commitment to inclusivity and innovation ensures that, with

every press, users can unlock a world of
possibilities that transcend the conventional
boundaries of smartphone interaction.

Chapter 7:

Camera Technology

Prepare to witness photography like never before as Apple unveils the iPhone 16 with enhanced camera features, headlined by a groundbreaking 48-megapixel Ultra Wide lens. In this era-defining moment, Apple redefines the boundaries of smartphone photography, offering users a visual experience that transcends imagination.

At the heart of the iPhone 16's camera innovation is the awe-inspiring 48-megapixel Ultra Wide lens. This technological marvel leverages pixel binning to combine data from four pixels into a single "super pixel," ensuring unparalleled image quality even in challenging lighting conditions. The result is a visual feast that captures every nuance, every detail, and every shade with breathtaking precision.

The 48-megapixel Ultra Wide lens isn't just a numbers game; it's a low-light mastery. With a lens structure featuring eight parts, including two glass elements and six plastic elements, this lens elevates low-light photography to new heights. Users can expect images that defy the constraints of darkness, delivering clarity, sharpness, and brilliance even in the most challenging environments.

The iPhone 16 Pro models are set to feature 5x Telephoto lenses, expanding the realm of optical zoom capabilities. This advancement ensures that users can capture distant subjects with incredible detail, bringing a professional touch to every photograph. The integration of 5x Telephoto lenses is a testament to Apple's commitment to pushing the boundaries of what is possible in smartphone photography.

Whether you choose the standard iPhone 16 or opt for the Pro models, the enhanced camera features, including the 48-megapixel Ultra Wide lens, promise a consistent and exceptional photography experience. Apple ensures that every user, irrespective of their chosen model, can explore the full potential of this revolutionary camera technology.

Beyond the sheer number of pixels, the iPhone 16's camera technology is a narrative of innovation. Apple's commitment to providing users with tools that transcend the ordinary extends to the camera's capabilities. From capturing stunning landscapes to detailed close-ups, the iPhone 16's camera becomes a creative companion for users who demand excellence in every shot.

Get ready to embark on a photographic journey where brilliance knows no bounds. The iPhone 16's camera features, anchored by the 48-megapixel Ultra Wide lens, invite users to explore, capture, and create visuals that redefine the art of smartphone photography.

Introduction of 5x Telephoto lenses for improved zoom capabilities

In a revolutionary leap forward, the iPhone 16 introduces 5x Telephoto lenses, elevating the smartphone photography experience to new heights. Prepare to be captivated by the power of optical zoom, as Apple redefines what's possible with the 5x Telephoto lenses featured in the Pro models.

The iPhone 16 Pro models mark a significant advancement in zoom capabilities with the integration of 5x Telephoto lenses. This optical marvel allows users to capture distant subjects with remarkable clarity and detail, bringing them closer to the action without compromising on image quality. It's not just a zoom; it's a visual journey that goes beyond the ordinary.

For photography enthusiasts and professionals alike, the 5x Telephoto lenses open up a world of creative possibilities. From capturing detailed landscapes to framing intricate details from a distance, the Pro models empower users to express their vision with precision and finesse. It's like having a professional camera in the palm of your hand.

Apple's commitment to delivering a consistent and exceptional photography experience extends to the implementation of 5x Telephoto lenses across the iPhone 16 Pro lineup. Whether you're exploring the capabilities of the Ultra Wide lens or zooming in with the Telephoto lens, the iPhone 16 Pro models ensure that every shot is a masterpiece.

The introduction of 5x Telephoto lenses is more than a technical achievement; it's a testament to Apple's relentless pursuit of innovation. By seamlessly integrating advanced optics into the iPhone 16 Pro models, Apple empowers users to explore the world of photography in ways they never thought possible.

While digital zoom has its limitations, the 5x Telephoto lenses bring optical precision to the forefront. Users can now capture moments with clarity and sharpness, even from a distance, without compromising on image quality. It's a leap beyond the digital boundaries, ensuring that every photo tells a story with unparalleled detail.

Prepare to experience photography in a new dimension as the iPhone 16 Pro models usher in the era of 5x Telephoto lenses. From breathtaking landscapes to detailed close-ups, the possibilities are as limitless as your imagination. Zoom into a world of optical mastery with the iPhone 16 Pro.

The potential inclusion of a periscope zoom lens for extended optical zoom

iPhone 16 pushes the boundaries of optical zoom with its groundbreaking Periscope Zoom Lens. Apple's relentless pursuit of innovation takes center stage, introducing extended optical zoom capabilities that redefine the way we capture the world around us.

The iPhone 16 introduces a game-changing feature – the Periscope Zoom Lens. Inspired by periscope mechanisms used in submarines, this groundbreaking technology enables an extended optical zoom range, allowing users to magnify distant subjects with exceptional clarity and detail. Get ready to explore new horizons and capture moments that were once beyond reach.

Traditional zoom lenses have their limitations, but the Periscope Zoom Lens transcends these boundaries. It utilizes a periscope arrangement to redirect light, enabling an extended focal length without compromising on device thickness. This innovative approach represents a leap forward in smartphone camera technology, ensuring that your creativity knows no bounds.

With the Periscope Zoom Lens, the iPhone 16 opens up new possibilities for photography enthusiasts and professionals alike. From photographing wildlife from a safe distance to capturing architectural details that were previously inaccessible, the extended optical zoom empowers users to see and capture the unseen. It's a window into worlds that were once distant and now brought close.

Apple's commitment to delivering a superior imaging experience is evident in the precision-engineered Periscope Zoom Lens. Every component is meticulously crafted to ensure optimal performance, providing users with a tool that goes beyond magnification – it captures moments with unparalleled sharpness and clarity. Each photo becomes a masterpiece, a testament to the synergy of technology and creativity.

The Periscope Zoom Lens is not just a technological marvel; it's a catalyst for creativity. As users explore the extended optical zoom capabilities, they are invited to reimagine their approach to photography. The iPhone 16 becomes a gateway to untold stories, allowing users to frame and capture the world in ways that were once reserved for professional lenses.

Prepare to revolutionize your photographic experience with the iPhone 16's Periscope Zoom Lens. Whether you're capturing the grandeur of landscapes or the intricacies of distant subjects, the extended optical zoom invites you to see beyond the obvious and revel in the art of visual storytelling.

Chapter 8:

Performance Upgrades

Dive into a new era of smartphone performance with the iPhone 16, where Apple's dedication to seamless functionality takes center stage. Anticipate a device that not only pushes the boundaries of technology but also addresses the age-old challenge of overheating. Let's explore the thermal improvements that ensure your iPhone 16 stays cool, even under the most demanding conditions.

The iPhone 16 introduces a cutting-edge thermal design centered around graphene, a material renowned for its exceptional thermal conductivity. This revolutionary system ensures efficient heat dissipation, allowing the device to maintain optimal operating temperatures during prolonged usage or resource-intensive tasks. Say goodbye to concerns about overheating, as the iPhone 16 sets a new standard for thermal performance.

Apple's engineers have strategically integrated the graphene thermal system to target heat at its source. Whether you're engaged in high-performance gaming, capturing stunning 4K videos, or multitasking with resource-intensive apps, the iPhone 16's thermal innovation actively manages heat generation. This ensures that the device remains cool and responsive, no matter how demanding your activities may be.

In addition to the graphene thermal system, the iPhone 16 Pro models are equipped with a metal battery casing. This advanced casing serves a dual purpose – not only does it enhance structural integrity, but it also contributes to improved heat dissipation. Apple's meticulous engineering ensures that the metal casing effectively mitigates heat buildup, further enhancing the iPhone 16's thermal efficiency.

The thermal improvements in the iPhone 16 are not merely about managing heat; they're about ensuring prolonged, uninterrupted performance. Whether you're streaming content, engaging in augmented reality experiences, or navigating graphics-intensive applications, the device remains cool, allowing you to focus on what matters most – enjoying the full capabilities of your iPhone 16.

Graphene's unique properties make it an ideal choice for thermal management in the iPhone 16. As a single layer of carbon atoms arranged in a hexagonal lattice, graphene exhibits exceptional thermal conductivity and mechanical strength. By harnessing the power of graphene, Apple has elevated the iPhone 16 to new heights, delivering a device that not only performs at its peak but does so with a level of thermal efficiency that ensures a consistently smooth user experience.

RAM upgrades for standard iPhone 16 models

In the heart of the iPhone 16, an upgrade to its internal powerhouse is expected. The standard iPhone 16 models are anticipated to receive a significant boost in RAM, with a move from the previous 6GB in the iPhone 15 models to a more robust 8GB configuration.

This leap in RAM capacity promises to elevate the device's overall performance, ensuring smoother multitasking, improved app responsiveness, and enhanced efficiency in handling resource-intensive tasks. As technology enthusiasts eagerly await the arrival of the iPhone 16 lineup, the prospect of an upgraded RAM is a testament to Apple's commitment to delivering cutting-edge user experiences.

Battery enhancements with stacked battery technology

Embracing innovation in power management, the iPhone 16 is rumored to feature cutting-edge advancements in battery technology. Apple is said to be adopting stacked battery technology for the iPhone 16 Pro models, introducing a revolutionary approach to battery design.

Stacked batteries, commonly employed in electric vehicles and medical devices, represent a leap forward in battery efficiency and lifespan. This technology enables a higher capacity within a more compact form, potentially translating to longer battery life and improved durability.

As Apple continues to push the boundaries of smartphone capabilities, the introduction of stacked battery technology in the iPhone 16 Pro models aims to address the ever-growing demands for sustained performance and prolonged device usage. With these advancements, users can anticipate a device that not only boasts powerful features but also delivers a longer-lasting and more reliable battery experience.

Chapter 9:

Release and Pricing

Mark your calendars, iPhone enthusiasts! The much-anticipated iPhone 16 models are expected to make their grand debut in September 2024. Following the tradition of Apple's annual fall releases, the iPhone 16 lineup is poised to capture the spotlight and set the tech world abuzz with excitement.

As September approaches, the anticipation for the unveiling of the latest iPhone models will reach a fever pitch. Apple aficionados and tech enthusiasts alike will eagerly await the official launch event, where the groundbreaking features, design innovations, and technological marvels of the iPhone 16 will be revealed in all their glory.

Stay tuned for the momentous occasion when Apple takes the stage to showcase the future of mobile technology with the iPhone 16. September 2024 promises to be a month of technological marvels, as Apple continues its legacy of pushing the boundaries and shaping the landscape of the smartphone industry.

Potential price adjustments based on increased production costs

As the countdown to the release of the iPhone 16 continues, there's more than just excitement in the air—there's also speculation about potential price adjustments. Industry insiders and analysts are keeping a close eye on the dynamics of component prices and production costs, which could influence the final pricing strategy for the iPhone 16 models.

With component prices for the standard iPhone 15 models already experiencing a record-high increase of 16 percent compared to the iPhone 14 models, there's a growing awareness that Apple may need to make strategic decisions to balance the books. While Apple absorbed the heightened production costs for the iPhone 15 lineup, the landscape could shift with the iPhone 16 launch.

As the tech giant navigates the intricate terrain of component pricing and production economics, the question on everyone's mind is whether the iPhone 16 models will see a price adjustment to maintain overall revenue. Apple's pricing decisions have a ripple effect on consumer expectations, and any adjustments will be keenly observed by both loyal iPhone users and potential buyers.

As we eagerly await the official pricing details, one thing is certain—the unveiling of the iPhone 16 models promises not only technological excellence but also intriguing insights into Apple's pricing strategies in response to the ever-evolving dynamics of the smartphone market. Stay tuned for updates on how Apple navigates this delicate balance between innovation and economic considerations.

Chapter 10:

Future iPhone Features

The anticipation for the upcoming iPhone 16 models is reaching a fever pitch, and enthusiasts are eager for a sneak peek into the potential features that might define Apple's next flagship devices. As the tech world buzzes with rumors and speculations, let's explore some of the exciting possibilities that could make the iPhone 16 series a groundbreaking addition to the Apple lineup.

1. RAM Upgrades: Industry insiders suggest that the standard iPhone 16 models could receive a significant boost in RAM, potentially upgrading from 6GB to 8GB. This enhancement aims to elevate the overall performance, allowing for smoother multitasking, faster app launches, and improved efficiency.

2. Stacked Battery Technology: Rumors are circulating about Apple incorporating stacked battery technology in the iPhone 16 Pro models. This innovation could result in higher capacity and a longer lifespan, signaling Apple's commitment to advancing battery performance in its flagship devices.

3. Cutting-Edge Camera Technology: The camera capabilities of the iPhone 16 series are expected to be nothing short of revolutionary. From a 48-megapixel Ultra Wide lens for enhanced low-light performance to the introduction of 5x Telephoto lenses for improved zoom capabilities, Apple is poised to redefine smartphone photography.

4. Thermal Improvements: Overheating concerns may become a thing of the past with the iPhone 16 models, thanks to a new thermal design that incorporates graphene technology. This thermal system aims to dissipate heat more efficiently, ensuring optimal performance even during resource-intensive tasks.

5. Advanced Connectivity: With the potential adoption of Wi-Fi 7 technology, the iPhone 16 Pro models could offer faster speeds and more reliable connectivity. Additionally, the transition to USB-C technology signifies Apple's commitment to enhanced connectivity standards.

6. 5G Modem Chips: The iPhone 16 series is expected to feature advanced 5G modem chips, with the Pro models potentially equipped with Qualcomm's Snapdragon X75 modem. This advancement promises faster and more efficient 5G connectivity, elevating the iPhone's capabilities in the era of high-speed data.

7. Price Adjustments: As component prices continue to fluctuate, there's speculation about potential price adjustments for the iPhone 16 models. Apple may need to navigate the delicate balance between offering cutting-edge technology and managing production costs, and consumers are eagerly awaiting the final pricing strategy.

While these features are based on rumors and early speculations, Apple's official unveiling is eagerly awaited to confirm the innovations that will shape the iPhone 16 series. As the launch date approaches, tech enthusiasts can look forward to an extraordinary blend of technology, design, and performance from Apple's latest flagship devices.

ProMotion technology for standard iPhone models starting in 2025

Looking into the future of iPhone models, there's a tantalizing possibility that ProMotion technology, known for its up to 120Hz refresh rates, could become a standard feature for iPhone models starting in 2025. Until then, ProMotion has been a hallmark feature limited to the higher-end "Pro" iPhones.

The introduction of ProMotion for standard iPhone models in 2025 promises a transformative visual experience for users. With its high refresh rates, ProMotion ensures smoother animations, more responsive touch interactions, and an overall heightened sense of fluidity in navigating through the device's interface.

This strategic move aligns with Apple's commitment to providing cutting-edge technology across its product range, allowing a broader audience to enjoy the benefits of ProMotion. Users can anticipate a more immersive and responsive display, enhancing their everyday interactions with the iPhone.

As Apple continues to push the boundaries of innovation, the integration of ProMotion into standard iPhone models signifies a commitment to democratizing advanced features. The year 2025 is poised to mark a significant shift in the iPhone lineup, bringing a premium display experience to a wider audience and setting new standards for smartphones in the years to come.

Speculations about under-display Face ID technology in 2025

As the tech world eagerly anticipates the future of iPhone models, one of the most intriguing speculations revolves around the possible introduction of under-display Face ID technology in 2025. This cutting-edge feature, which has been a subject of numerous rumors and discussions, holds the promise of revolutionizing the way users interact with their iPhones.

The concept of under-display Face ID involves embedding facial recognition sensors directly beneath the iPhone's display, eliminating the need for a visible camera cutout or notch. This innovation not only contributes to a sleeker and more seamless design but also maximizes the usable display space, providing users with a more immersive visual experience.

While initial rumors hinted at the possibility of under-display Face ID debuting earlier, updated information now suggests that users might need to wait until 2025 or later for this transformative technology. Despite the extended timeline, the anticipation surrounding under-display Face ID remains high, with users excited about the potential for a bezel-less and camera-free display.

Apple's commitment to refining and perfecting features before integration aligns with its reputation for delivering high-quality and innovative products. If and when under-display Face ID becomes a reality, it will likely represent a milestone in smartphone design, setting new standards for aesthetics and functionality. As the tech landscape evolves, Apple continues to fuel excitement and speculation about the future capabilities of its iconic iPhone lineup.

Conclusion

In the ever-evolving landscape of technology, the anticipation surrounding the upcoming iPhone 16 series has reached unprecedented heights. This book has taken you on a captivating journey, exploring the rumors, speculations, and potential innovations that could shape the future of Apple's iconic iPhone lineup.

As we eagerly await the official unveiling of the iPhone 16, the tech community is abuzz with excitement, envisioning the possibilities that each speculated feature brings to the table. From the larger display sizes to the introduction of novel technologies like under-display Face ID, the iPhone 16 promises to be a groundbreaking addition to the Apple family.

Your engagement in this exploration of the iPhone 16 series is a testament to your curiosity and enthusiasm for cutting-edge technology. The world of smartphones is on the brink of another transformative chapter, and Apple, with its commitment to innovation, is poised to redefine our expectations.

As you turn the pages of this book and look forward to the future, we invite you to share your thoughts and predictions in the comments section. What are your expectations for the iPhone 16? Which rumored feature has captured your imagination the most? Your insights and opinions contribute to the collective excitement of the tech community.

Join the conversation, be a part of the speculation, and let your voice be heard. Your reviews and comments are not just reflections of your anticipation but also valuable contributions to the ongoing dialogue about the next generation of iPhones. Thank you for being a part of this journey, and may the iPhone 16 series bring innovation, delight, and technological marvels beyond our wildest imaginations.

www.ingramcontent.com/pod-product-compliance
Lightning Source LLC
LaVergne TN
LVHW051737050326
832903LV00023B/965